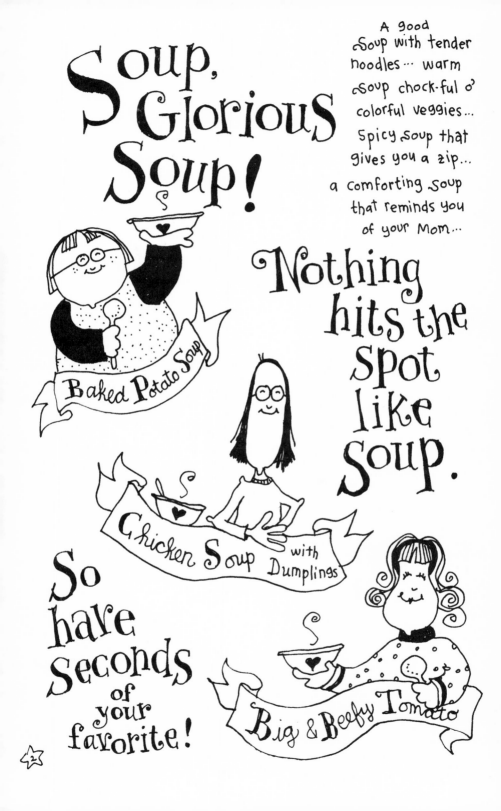

Soup, Glorious Soup!

A good soup with tender noodles... warm soup chock-ful o' colorful veggies... spicy soup that gives you a zip... a comforting soup that reminds you of your Mom...

Nothing hits the spot like Soup.

So have seconds of your favorite!

Baked Potato Soup

Chicken Soup with Dumplings

Big & Beefy Tomato

2

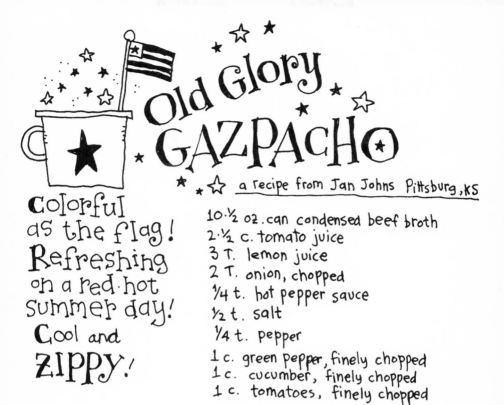

Old Glory GAZPACHO

a recipe from Jan Johns Pittsburg, KS

Colorful as the flag! Refreshing on a red·hot summer day! Cool and ZIPPY!

10.½ oz. can condensed beef broth
2.½ c. tomato juice
3 T. lemon juice
2 T. onion, chopped
¼ t. hot pepper sauce
½ t. salt
¼ t. pepper
1 c. green pepper, finely chopped
1 c. cucumber, finely chopped
1 c. tomatoes, finely chopped

In a jar, combine first 7 ingredients. Cover and shake well. Chill for 4 hours. Place mixture in freezer for one hour, but do not allow it to freeze. Chill the chopped veggies and divide into 8 different serving dishes ～ clear mugs are pretty! Pour soup over veggies and serve immediately.

★ Just for Fun, spear a chunk of tomato on a tiny American flag toothpick and add it to the soup mug for an OLD GLORY touch ～ GRAND! ★

Life never becomes a habit to me. It's always a marvel.
— Katherine Mansfield

3

Cool as a Cuke SOUP

a recipe from
Kelley Robinson
Topeka, KS

...delicious on a steamy day!

2 medium cucumbers, peeled, seeded & finely grated
1 qt. buttermilk
1 T. snipped green onion
1 t. salt
garnish: snipped parsley

Mix cucumbers, buttermilk and green onions together. Cover and chill about 4 hours. Mix in salt and garnish before serving. Serves 6 to 8.

ALOHA CHILI

a recipe from Donna Nowicki
Center City, MN

1 onion, finely chopped
1 T. olive oil
15½ oz. can kidney beans, rinsed & drained
16 oz. can pork & beans
20 oz. can crushed pineapple
1 c. catsup
¼ c. brown sugar, packed
¼ c. vinegar

Sauté onion in olive oil 'til tender & golden. Stir in remaining ingredients, cover and simmer for 20 minutes. Makes 6 to 8 servings.

4

BIG and Beefy Tomato Soup

a recipe from Debbie Bishop   Winston, OR

1 lb. ground beef
1 c. onions, chopped
2 c. carrots, sliced
14.½ oz. can green beans
15.¼ oz. can corn
3 stalks celery, chopped
14.½ oz. can Italian stewed tomatoes
15 oz. can tomato sauce
2 t. sugar
1 t. celery seeds
Salt & pepper to taste

Brown ground beef in large saucepan; drain. Add onions, carrots, green beans, corn, celery & tomatoes. Stir in tomato sauce, sugar, celery seeds, salt & pepper. Simmer covered for 30 minutes, stirring occasionally. Makes 8 to 10 servings.

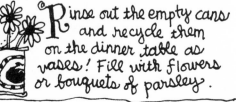

Rinse out the empty cans and recycle them on the dinner table as vases! Fill with flowers or bouquets of parsley.

SOUP ETIQUETTE
by Kate.

DON'T test the heat of soup by dipping in a big toe. OW.

DON'T lick the empty bowl unless no one is looking.

DON'T put your face in the bowl.

5

Vegetarian Garden Patch CHILI

a recipe from Robbin Chamberlain
Worthington, OH

1 T. vegetable oil
3 onions, chopped
1 carrot, peeled & chopped
1 T. jalapeño pepper, chopped
4 cloves garlic, minced
3 to 4 t. chili powder
2 t. cumin
28·oz. can plus 14·oz. can stewed tomatoes, undrained
4 t. sugar
2 15·oz. cans kidney beans, drained & rinsed
⅓ c. bulger wheat, uncooked
Salt & pepper, to taste

Heat oil in a large saucepan or Dutch oven. Add onions, carrot, pepper, garlic, chili powder & cumin. Cook, stirring occasionally, over medium-high heat for about 5 minutes. Add tomatoes & sugar; continue cooking about 5 minutes, stirring occasionally. Reduce heat to low and mix in beans & bulger wheat. Simmer 'til thickened, about 15 minutes. Makes 4 servings.

Farm: What a city man dreams of at 5 p.m., never at 5 a.m. — anonymous

Vickie's Farmer's Potato Soup

... great after a fall day in the garden!

2 leeks, thinly sliced
1 onion, sliced
2 T. butter
1·½ qts. chicken broth
4 potatoes, peeled & sliced
salt to taste
1 T. fresh thyme
½ c. heavy cream
Garnish: 1 c. cheddar cheese, grated
½ c. bacon, crisply cooked & crumbled

Sauté leeks and onion in butter until softened, but not brown. Add broth, potatoes, salt & thyme. Simmer for 40 minutes, stirring frequently to avoid scorching. Add cream, stir and bring to a boil. Remove heat and garnish with cheese and bacon. Makes 8 servings.

O, Lord, how manifold are thy works! In wisdom hast thou made them all: the earth is full of thy riches. – PSALMS 104:24

TATER

7

QUICK!
Chicken
CHILI

a recipe from Becky Newton
Oklahoma City, OK

3 whole boneless, skinless
    chicken breasts, chopped
1 c. onion, chopped
1 green pepper, chopped
2 cloves garlic, minced
2 T. oil
2 14·½ oz. cans stewed tomatoes
15·½ oz. can pinto beans, drained
2/3 to 3/4 c. picante sauce
1 t. chili powder
1 t. cumin
½ t. seasoning salt

Cook chicken, onion, green
pepper, garlic & oil
together in a large saucepan.
Add tomatoes, pinto beans,
picante sauce, chili powder,
cumin & seasoning
salt. Simmer for
20 minutes.
Serves 6 to 8.

CHILI WAGON

It is astonishing
how short a time
it takes for very
wonderful things
to happen. - Frances Hodgson
                        Burnett

8

Texas Tortilla Soup

a recipe from Jeannine English
Wylie, TX

4 chicken breasts, cooked & cubed
1·1/4 oz. pkg. taco seasoning
1/4 c. onion, chopped
3 14·1/2 oz. cans stewed
        tomatoes
14·1/2 oz. can chicken broth
15·oz. can hominy, drained
16·oz. can pinto beans, drained
16·oz. can Great Northern
        beans, drained
4·oz. can green chilies
Garnish: Cheddar cheese
        & tortilla strips

Mix all ingredients together
    in a stockpot. Simmer
for about 30 minutes, then
garnish. Makes 10 to
12 servings.

Bless My. Stars. and. garters. it's good!

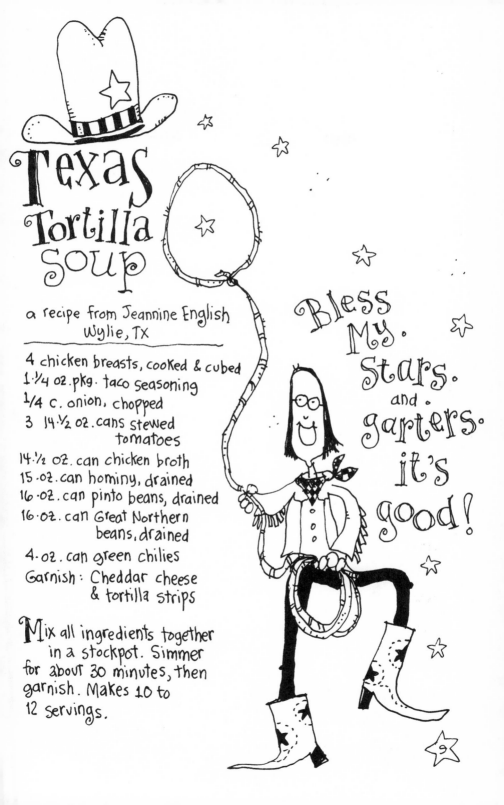

Tacorrific Soup

...great with ice-cold root beer and oven-warm corn bread!

a recipe from Diana Roper   Hammon, OK

2 lbs. ground beef
1 onion, chopped
8-oz. can chopped green chilies
14-½ oz. can stewed tomatoes
16-oz. can Ranch-style beans, drained
15-¼ oz. can corn

1-½ c. water
14-½ oz. can tomatoes
1-¼ oz. pkg. taco seasoning
1-oz. pkg. ranch dressing mix
1 t. salt
½ t. pepper

Brown beef & onion together in a large saucepan; drain. Add remaining ingredients ⌐simmer for 30 minutes. Makes 6 servings.

6 GOOD THINGS TO EAT WITH SOUP

A SIMPLE GREEN SALAD

SLICES OF FRESH FRUIT

GOOD CRUSTY BREAD

CHUNKS OF CHEESE

LOTS OF SALTY CRACKERS

PIE, of course

"Indeed, to be simple is to be great." — RALPH WALDO EMERSON

Late Afternoon Soup

a recipe from
Rachel Reilly
Columbia, SC

Spend the afternoon doing something fun, then cook up a pot of this quick & yummy gumbo!

2 c. boneless, skinless chicken breast, chopped

2 c. okra, sliced

2 8-oz. cans chicken broth

1 c. water

14·½ oz. can diced tomatoes

1 onion, chopped

1 stalk celery, thinly sliced

½ green pepper, chopped

¼ t. garlic powder

1 t. Cajun seasoning

1 c. instant rice, uncooked

Salt & pepper to taste

Combine all ingredients in a stockpot, except for the rice. Bring to a boil and simmer, covered, 15 minutes or until juices in chicken run clear. Add rice and simmer an additional 15 minutes. Makes 6 servings.

The secret of my vigor is that I have managed to have a lot of fun.

— Lowell Thomas —

Soup and Sandwich ~
a match made in heaven!

OUR FAVORITES:

♥ CHICKEN NOODLE ✝ PEANUT BUTTER & JELLY

♥ TOMATO ✝ GRILLED CHEESE

♥ BROCCOLI CHEESE SOUP ✝ TURKEY on WHEAT

♥ VEGGIE ✝ HAM on WHITE

Cheesy Italiano Soup

...smells incredibly good on the stove!

1 ¼ c. mushrooms, sliced
½ c. onion, finely chopped
1 T. oil
2 c. water
15-oz. can pizza sauce
1 c. pepperoni, chopped
1 c. tomatoes, chopped
½ c. Italian sausage, cooked
¼ t. Italian seasoning
¼ c. grated Parmesan cheese
Garnish: shredded mozzarella cheese

Sauté mushrooms & onion in oil for 2 to 3 minutes or until tender. Add water, pizza sauce, pepperoni, tomatoes, sausage & Italian seasoning. Bring to boil over medium heat, then reduce heat and simmer, covered, for 20 minutes. Stir in parmesan cheese and garnish with mozzarella. Serves 4.

a recipe from Becky Sykes · Gooseberry Patch

Quick ✱ Chick Noodly Soup

...For when you're hungry this very minute!

a recipe from
Deana Kail   Carrollton, OH

46-oz. can chicken broth
½ lb. boneless, skinless chicken, cubed
½ c. med. egg noodles, uncooked
1 c. carrots, sliced
½ c. onion, chopped
⅓ c. celery, sliced
1 t. dried dill weed
¼ t. pepper

SOUP ♥

comes into its own, poor-man style, as a main course. One small serving of a ravishing soup is *infuriating!* It is like seeing the *Pearly Gates* swing shut in one's face after one glimpse of **HEAVEN.**

- MARJORIE KINNANS RAWLINGS-
(CROSS CREEK COOKERY 1942)

Combine broth, chicken, noodles, carrots, onions & seasonings. Bring to a boil, then reduce heat and simmer for 20 minutes or 'til noodles are tender.
Makes 8 servings.

Time STAYS LONG ENOUGH FOR ANYONE WHO WILL USE IT. ~ Leonardo DaVinci

13

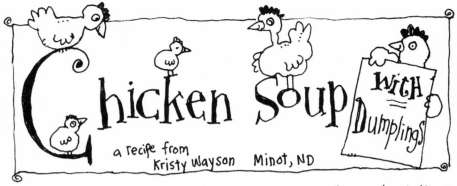

Chicken Soup with Dumplings

a recipe from
Kristy Wayson   Minot, ND

1 chicken
3 to 4 stalks celery, diced

3 to 4 carrots, peeled & sliced
5 to 6 chicken bouillon cubes

Combine chicken, celery & carrots in a large stock pot; cover with water. Bring to a boil ～ continue to cook until chicken is tender and juices run clear. Add additional water if needed. Mix in bouillon cubes, stirring to dissolve. Remove chicken from broth and place in a covered baking dish to keep warm. When cool enough to handle, remove and chop meat. Bring broth to a boil, add meat and dumplings. Makes 8 to 10 servings.

Dumplings:

4 eggs
2 c. all-purpose flour
12 T. water

Mix eggs & flour with enough water to form a soft dough. Drop dumplings in boiling broth. Cook 15 minutes after broth returns to a full boil.

GOOD SOUP

Serve it Up!

me and thee Onion Soup

a recipe from
Darlene Caldwell   Portland, OR

Who says you must eat soup out of a bowl? Try these clever serving ideas to add a little zip to meal time!

Alphabet soup in a banana split dish spells F-U-N for kids (and may persuade them to eat a little more if they're picky).

Cold soup like gazpacho or fruity refreshers taste cool in a margarita or martini glass ∽ garnish with fresh veggies or fruit chunks on a "umbrella" toothpick for the silliness of it!

Make a hearty meal from stew in a big old mug ∽ or serve a dainty portion of rich consommé in a tiny teacup or cappuccino cup.

2 c. onion, thinly sliced
2 t. butter
1 t. all-purpose flour
3 c. beef broth
2 slices French bread, lightly toasted
½ c. shredded Swiss cheese
½ c. grated Parmesan cheese

Sauté onions in butter until tender. Whisk in flour and continue to cook 5 minutes. Stir in broth and bring soup to a boil. Reduce heat and simmer for 15 minutes. Divide soup between 2 oven-proof bowls and top each with a slice of bread. Sprinkle bread with cheeses and heat under the broiler 'til Swiss cheese is melted and golden.
    Makes 2 servings.

a gift of Soup

Fill an over-sized mug with instant soup packages and plastic spoons for a co-worker's break-time treat.

An invitation to dinner is a gift in itself! Tie an invitation to a spoon with a pretty ribbon, and hand-deliver to friends & neighbors.

A jar of homemade soup and all the goodies to go with it : crackers, croutons, breads & muffins ～ a basketful of yumminess for a housewarming or new parents!

A nice thermos full of delicious hot soup and fresh-baked rolls wrapped up in a neat towel make a tummy-warming present for a friend embarking on a journey or someone working outdoors.

HOW MUCH SOUP?

An Appetizer-portion of soup is about 3/4 to 1 full cup; A main course portion might run from 1 1/4 to 2 cups of soup.

16

We make A living by what we get ～ we make a life by WHAT we give.

— Winston Churchill —

GREAT GARNISH!

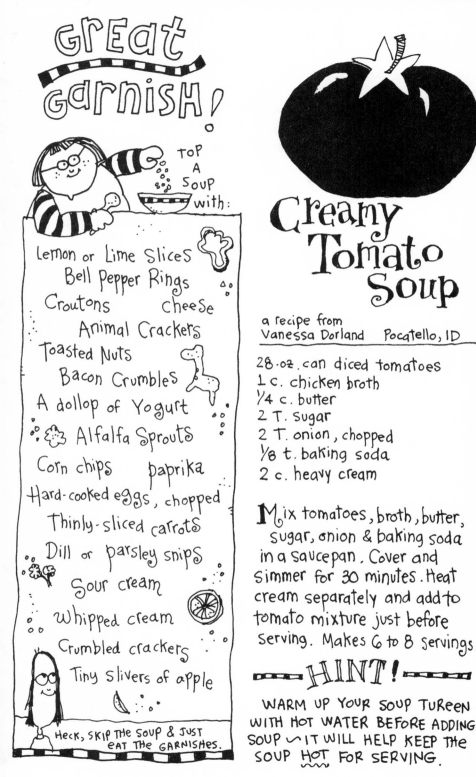

TOP A SOUP with:

- Lemon or Lime Slices
- Bell Pepper Rings
- Croutons
- Cheese
- Animal Crackers
- Toasted Nuts
- Bacon Crumbles
- A dollop of Yogurt
- Alfalfa Sprouts
- Corn chips
- Paprika
- Hard-cooked eggs, chopped
- Thinly-sliced carrots
- Dill or parsley snips
- Sour cream
- Whipped cream
- Crumbled crackers
- Tiny slivers of apple

Heck, skip the soup & just eat the garnishes.

Creamy Tomato Soup

a recipe from
Vanessa Dorland   Pocatello, ID

28-oz. can diced tomatoes
1 c. chicken broth
1/4 c. butter
2 T. sugar
2 T. onion, chopped
1/8 t. baking soda
2 c. heavy cream

Mix tomatoes, broth, butter, sugar, onion & baking soda in a saucepan. Cover and simmer for 30 minutes. Heat cream separately and add to tomato mixture just before serving. Makes 6 to 8 servings.

HINT!

WARM UP YOUR SOUP TUREEN WITH HOT WATER BEFORE ADDING SOUP — IT WILL HELP KEEP THE SOUP HOT FOR SERVING.

ITALIAN Wedding Soup

a recipe from
John Alexander   New Britain, CT

1 whole chicken
4 c. water
½ c. onion, finely chopped
1 bunch endive, finely chopped
1 c. cocktail vegetable juice
1 lb. ground beef
1 egg
¼ c. grated Parmesan cheese
Salt & pepper to taste
⅛ t. dried oregano

Place chicken in a Dutch oven, add enough water to cover and bring to a boil. Simmer until chicken is tender and juices run clear, about one hour. Bone chicken and cut into small cubes. Return chicken to broth — add veggies and vegetable juice. Heat to a simmer. Combine ground beef, egg, cheese & spices. Shape into one-inch balls and drop into simmering soup. Cook slowly over low heat 'til vegetables are tender and meatballs are fully cooked. Makes 4 to 6 delicious servings.

I do.

I Love it, Love it, Love it!

To make good soup, the pot must only simmer, or "smile."
— French proverb —

Magic Pumpkin ✶ Apple Soup

a recipe from Tori Willis ✶ Champaign, Il

¼ c. butter
1 clove garlic, minced
1 onion, chopped
1 leek, chopped
1 apple, peeled & chopped
1 T. curry powder

2 c. fresh pumpkin, chopped
4 c. chicken broth
1 c. whipping cream
Salt & pepper to taste

Melt butter in saucepan; stir in garlic, onion, leek and apple. Sauté until onion & apple are tender. Stir in curry powder — cook one minute, stirring constantly. Add pumpkin & chicken broth. Bring to a boil, stirring occasionally. Reduce heat & simmer 'til vegetables are tender. Puree mixture in a blender or food processor. Return to saucepan — stir in cream. Season with salt & pepper. Makes 6 to 8 servings.

♪ MAGICAL TASTE!

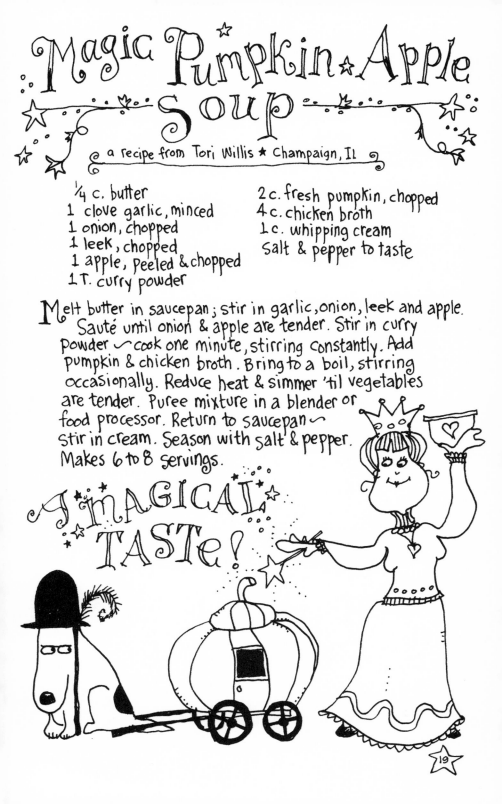

Butternut Squash Soup

a recipe from Tina Stidam
Delaware, OH

2·½ lbs. butternut squash, halved, seeded, peeled & cubed

2 c. leeks, chopped

2 Granny Smith apples, peeled, cored & diced

2 14.½ oz. cans chicken broth

1 c. water

Seasoned salt & white pepper, to taste

Garnish: fresh parsley

Combine squash, leeks, apples, broth & water in a 4·quart slow cooker. Cover and cook on low for 6 to 7 hours or until squash and leeks are tender. Increase temperature to high heat. Carefully purée the hot soup, in 3 or 4 batches, in a food processor or blender until smooth. Return the puréed soup to the slow cooker. Season with salt and pepper. Cover and continue to cook on high heat an additional 30 minutes. Garnish with parsley. Serves 8.

❤

Good has two meanings; it means that which is good absolutely and that which is good for somebody. — ARISTOTLE

SOUP DISASTER?

Of course, it's not YOUR fault — blame it on "BUCKLICH MENNLI", the bane of every kitchen! According to Pennsylvania Dutch lore, this little hump-backed elf is responsible for all kinds of kitchen mischief, from burned cakes to broken crocks and ruined soups.

Baked Potato Soup

a recipe from Myra Baker
Harrisonburg, VA

2/3 c. butter
2/3 c. all-purpose flour
7 c. milk
4 potatoes, baked, peeled
     and cubed
4 green onions, diced
12 bacon slices, crisply
     cooked and crumbled

1·¼ c. Cheddar cheese,
     shredded
8 oz. sour cream
3/4 t. salt
½ t. pepper

Melt butter in a Dutch oven. Stir in flour and whisk over medium heat until smooth. Gradually add milk, stirring constantly until thickened. Add potatoes and onions. Bring to a boil, stirring constantly. Reduce heat ⌐ simmer for 10 minutes. Add remaining ingredients, stirring until cheese is melted. Makes 6 to 8 servings.

URK!!
WHAT TO DO WHEN SOUP IS JUST TOO SALTY!

Simply cut a peeled raw potato into big chunks and drop in the soup pot. Leave it there for several minutes then remove it. Still too salty? Add a little bit of sugar to the soup!

21

Friends' Broccoli and Cheese SOUP

a Yummy Recipe from Melody Mayo * Ridgely, MD

6 c. water
10-oz. pkg. frozen, chopped broccoli
1 onion, chopped
8 oz. pasteurized process cheese spread, cubed
2 t. pepper
½ to 3/4 t. salt
½ t. garlic powder
1 c. milk
1 c. half-and-half
¼ c. butter
½ c. all-purpose flour
½ c. cold water

Bring 6 cups water to a boil in a Dutch oven; add broccoli & onion. Reduce heat and simmer, uncovered, for 10 minutes. Add cheese & seasonings ~stir 'til cheese melts. Stir in milk, half-and-half and butter; simmer 'til heated through. Combine flour & cold water, stirring 'til smooth. Gradually add to broccoli mixture, stirring constantly. Cook over medium heat 'til thickened. Makes 6 to 8 servings.

22

I enjoyed the mealtimes more than the meals. —MURIEL SPARKS

CAJUN CORN SOUP

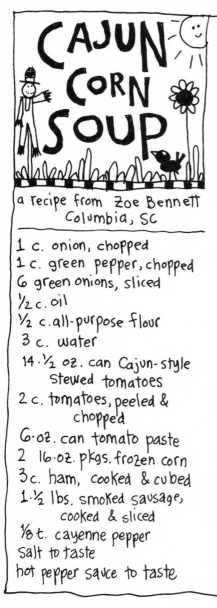

a recipe from Zoe Bennett
Columbia, SC

1 c. onion, chopped
1 c. green pepper, chopped
6 green onions, sliced
½ c. oil
½ c. all-purpose flour
3 c. water
14·½ oz. can Cajun-style stewed tomatoes
2 c. tomatoes, peeled & chopped
6-oz. can tomato paste
2 16-oz. pkgs. frozen corn
3 c. ham, cooked & cubed
1·½ lbs. smoked sausage, cooked & sliced
⅛ t. cayenne pepper
Salt to taste
hot pepper sauce to taste

Saute onion, green pepper & green onions together in oil until tender ~about 5 minutes. Add flour, stir & cook 'til bubbly. Blend in water, tomatoes & tomato paste and mix well. Stir in corn, ham, sausage, pepper, salt & hot pepper sauce. Bring to a boil ~ stir frequently. Reduce heat and simmer, uncovered, for one hour, stirring occasionally. Makes 12 to 14 servings.

To like and dislike the same things, that is indeed true friendship.

— SALLUST —
86-34 B.C.

To remove fat from soup:

refrigerate and remove the congealed layer from the top... OR, place several lettuce leaves on top of soup as it's cooking... they'll absorb some of the extra fat!

good for you BAKED STEW

a recipe from
Holly Sutton   Middleburgh, NY

2 10-3/4 oz. cans mushroom soup
1·½ lbs. smoked Kielbasa,
            chopped
5 potatoes, peeled & chopped
4 carrots, peeled & sliced
3 onions, chopped
1 c. green beans
3/4 lb. mushrooms, halved

Combine all ingredients in a
   13"x9" baking dish. Cover
with foil and bake at 350
degrees for 1·¼ hours.
Stir and bake an additional
30 minutes, uncovered, or until
veggies are tender. Makes
6 servings.

B.Y.O. Spoon!
Hearty Ham & Bean Soup

a recipe from Lori Rehrig
Mohrsville, PA

1 lb. mixed dried beans
2 T. salt
1 lb. ham, cooked & chopped
1 c. celery, diced
1 c. potatoes, diced
1 onion, chopped
1 c. carrots, diced
1·lb. can diced tomatoes
1 t. chili powder
salt & pepper to taste

Wash beans — pour into a
   large stockpot. Cover
with 2 inches of water,
add salt & soak overnight.
Drain beans, discard water
and return to stockpot. Cover
with 2 quarts water, bring
to a boil and simmer for
3 hours. Add ham & remaining
ingredients; simmer for 1
hour or 'til beans are
tender. Makes 8 to 10
delicious servings so ask
friends to join you!

I·SPY· Pepperoni soup

a recipe from Laura Petrillo
Riverside, CA

SIT DOWN WITH A BOWL OF THIS SPICY SOUP and A GOOD SPY NOVEL! ~the perfect lunch time combination~

28·oz·can Italian·style crushed tomatoes

2 15·oz·cans beef broth

2 15·oz·cans Great Northern beans, drained

2 6·oz·sticks pepperoni, sliced

1 c. pasta shells, uncooked

Combine crushed tomatoes, broth, beans & pepperoni in a large saucepan; bring to a boil. Add pasta, cook over medium heat for 10 to 12 minutes or until pasta is tender. Makes 6 to 8 servings.

NOW THIS is SOUP WORTH SLURPing.

25

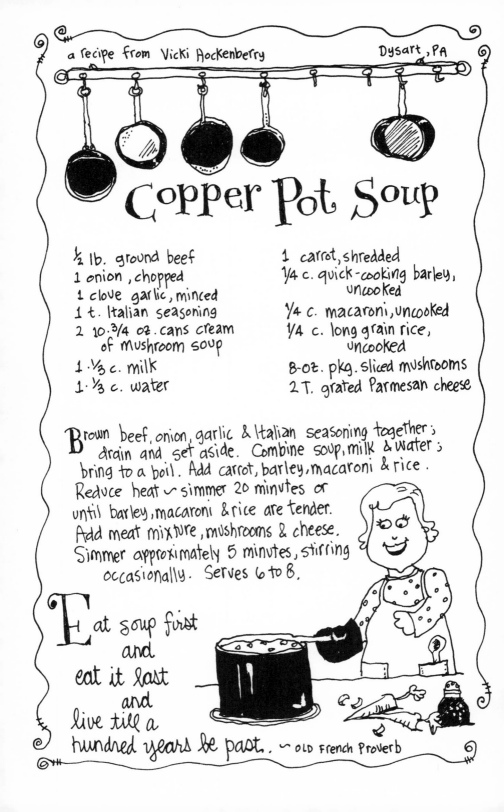

Copper Pot Soup

½ lb. ground beef
1 onion, chopped
1 clove garlic, minced
1 t. Italian seasoning
2 10.¾ oz. cans cream
   of mushroom soup
1·⅓ c. milk
1·⅓ c. water

1 carrot, shredded
¼ c. quick-cooking barley,
          uncooked
¼ c. macaroni, uncooked
¼ c. long grain rice,
          uncooked
8-oz. pkg. sliced mushrooms
2 T. grated Parmesan cheese

Brown beef, onion, garlic & Italian seasoning together; drain and set aside. Combine soup, milk & water; bring to a boil. Add carrot, barley, macaroni & rice. Reduce heat — simmer 20 minutes or until barley, macaroni & rice are tender. Add meat mixture, mushrooms & cheese. Simmer approximately 5 minutes, stirring occasionally. Serves 6 to 8.

Eat soup first
   and
eat it last
   and
live till a
hundred years be past. — OLD French Proverb

Tom Turkey Stew

...invite your Thanksgiving leftovers to lunch!

a recipe from Kris Saia
★ Topeka, Ks

4 c. chicken broth
1 c. water
3 bay leaves
1 lg. onion, chopped
1 lg. carrot, chopped
2 cloves garlic, minced
leftover turkey meat,
   boneless & skinless
1 c. bowtie pasta

In large saucepan, bring broth & water to a boil. Add bay leaves & veggies ⌇ simmer, uncovered, 10 minutes. Add garlic, meat & pasta. Simmer an additional 10 minutes until pasta is tender. Remove bay leaf before serving. Makes 3 servings.

The beauty of this recipe is like that of most soups ⌇ **Experiment!** You can add all kinds of yummy leftovers to the pot & it just gets better.

SPOT

Left ★ Over Soup? Oh, Boy!

Almost all soups keep well and improve with age ⌇ except those made with fish or seafood. Refrigerate leftovers and cover tightly. Soups made with meat, fruit, milk, poultry, cream & eggs will keep for 2 to 3 days in the fridge ⌇ those made purely with veggies or beans will be good for 3 days. Freeze up to 1 month, then thaw frozen soup in the refrigerator.

Fireside Veggie Soup

a recipe from Cyndy Rogers
Upton, MA

2 T. onion, chopped
1 T. margarine
1 c. frozen corn
½ c. broccoli, chopped
¼ c. carrot, shredded
¼ c. water

10.3/4 oz. can cream of potato soup
1 c. milk
¼ c. Cheddar cheese, shredded
1 oz. Provolone cheese, cubed
⅛ t. pepper

Saute onion in margarine 'til tender but not brown. Add corn, broccoli, carrot & water. Bring to a boil, then reduce heat and simmer, covered, for 10 minutes or until veggies are tender. Stir in soup, milk, cheeses & pepper. Cook and stir over medium heat 'til cheese is melted & soup is heated through. Serves 4.

Put on your jammies, wrap up in a quilt and eat soup by the fire!

FROSTY DAY CLAM CHOWDER

a heart-warming recipe from Karen Hess ★ Scott City, KS

2 6.5-oz cans minced clams, drained & juice reserved

1 c. carrots, grated
1 c. onion, finely chopped
1 c. celery, chopped
2 c. potatoes, diced
3/4 c. butter
3/4 c. all-purpose flour
1½ t. salt
1/8 t. pepper
1/2 t. sugar
1 qt. half-and-half

Pour clam juice in a saucepan, add vegetables & enough water to barely cover the veggies. Simmer about 1 hour or 'til veggies are tender. Melt butter in a large stockpot; stir in flour & seasonings. Cook until bubbly, then whisk in half-and-half. Add undrained vegetables & clams. Heat through but do not boil. Makes 8 servings.

More, please!

Kate's CLUB Sandwich

"It's the BEST friend a bowl of soup ever had."

4 slices of toast
Raspberry Jelly
Lettuce
Sliced turkey & ham
Crisp Bacon Slices

Spread the jelly on the toast. Add a piece of lettuce, then just start piling up the layers, the taller the better. Stretch mouth open and wedge monster sandwich inside. Alternate bites with soup. Take long, digestive nap afterwards.

JoAnn's HOT & SOUR SOUP

...makes your mouth go WOW·EE!

1 potato
3 c. chicken broth
3 ginger root slices
1 carrot, peeled & diced
1 stalk celery, diced
1 jalapeño pepper, cored, seeded & minced
zest & juice of 1 lime
1 boneless, skinless chicken breast, thinly sliced
1 t. soy sauce
¼ c. green onions, minced

Place potato in a 2-quart saucepan, cover with water and boil until tender. Peel & dice potato; set aside. Combine chicken broth, ginger root, carrot, celery, jalapeño & lime zest. Simmer until carrots are tender ~ about 20 minutes. Add chicken, potato, lime juice, soy sauce & green onions. Simmer 5 to 10 minutes or until chicken slices are cooked through. Discard ginger before serving. Makes 2 servings.

Cute Croutons!

A lovely little touch that only takes a minute or 2 extra!

Butter bread slices and cut into shapes using cookie cutters. Heat on a cookie sheet at 425° 'til toasty and crisp.

Fall Delight

...positively delicious after an autumn day spent raking leaves!

a recipe from
Shaney Smith

Gilbert, AZ

1 onion, chopped
2 T. oil
2 lbs. ground beef
2 T. soy sauce
2 T. brown sugar
4-oz. can sliced mushrooms

10.3/4 oz. can cream of chicken soup
1·½ c. rice, cooked
8-oz. can sliced water chestnuts
1 pumpkin, seeded & cleaned, reserve top with stem

Sauté onion & oil in a saucepan until onion is soft. Add ground beef; brown & drain. Stir in soy sauce, brown sugar, mushrooms & soup. Simmer, uncovered, for 10 minutes. Add rice & water chestnuts; blend well. Set pumpkin on a baking sheet ~ spoon beef mixture inside. Replace pumpkin top and bake at 350 degrees for one hour. Serve from the pumpkin. Serves 6 to 8.

SOUPS!

ALOHA CHILI 4
BAKED POTATO SOUP 21
BIG & BEEFY TOMATO SOUP 5
BUTTERNUT SQUASH SOUP 20
CAJUN CORN SOUP 23
CHEESY ITALIANO SOUP 12
CHICKEN CHILI 8
CHICKEN SOUP WITH DUMPLINGS 14
COOL·AS·A·CUKE SOUP 4
COPPER POT SOUP 26
CREAMY TOMATO SOUP 17
CUTE CROUTONS 30
FALL DELIGHT 31
FIRESIDE VEGGIE SOUP 28
FRIENDS' BROCCOLI & CHEESE SOUP 22
FROSTY DAY CLAM CHOWDER 29
GOOD FOR YOU BAKED STEW 24
HEARTY HAM & BEAN SOUP 24
I SPY PEPPERONI SOUP 25
ITALIAN WEDDING SOUP 18
JOANN'S HOT & SOUR SOUP 30
KATE'S CLUB SANDWICH 29
LATE AFTERNOON SOUP 11
MAGIC PUMPKIN & APPLE SOUP 19
ME & THEE ONION SOUP 15
OLD GLORY GAZPACHO 3
QUICK·CHICK NOODLY SOUP 13
TACORRIFIC SOUP 10
TEXAS TORTILLA SOUP 9
TOM TURKEY STEW 27
VEGETARIAN GARDEN PATCH CHILI 6
VICKIE'S FARMER'S POTATO SOUP 7

I find that a great part of the information I have was acquired by looking up something and finding something else on the way. —FRANKLIN P. ADAMS